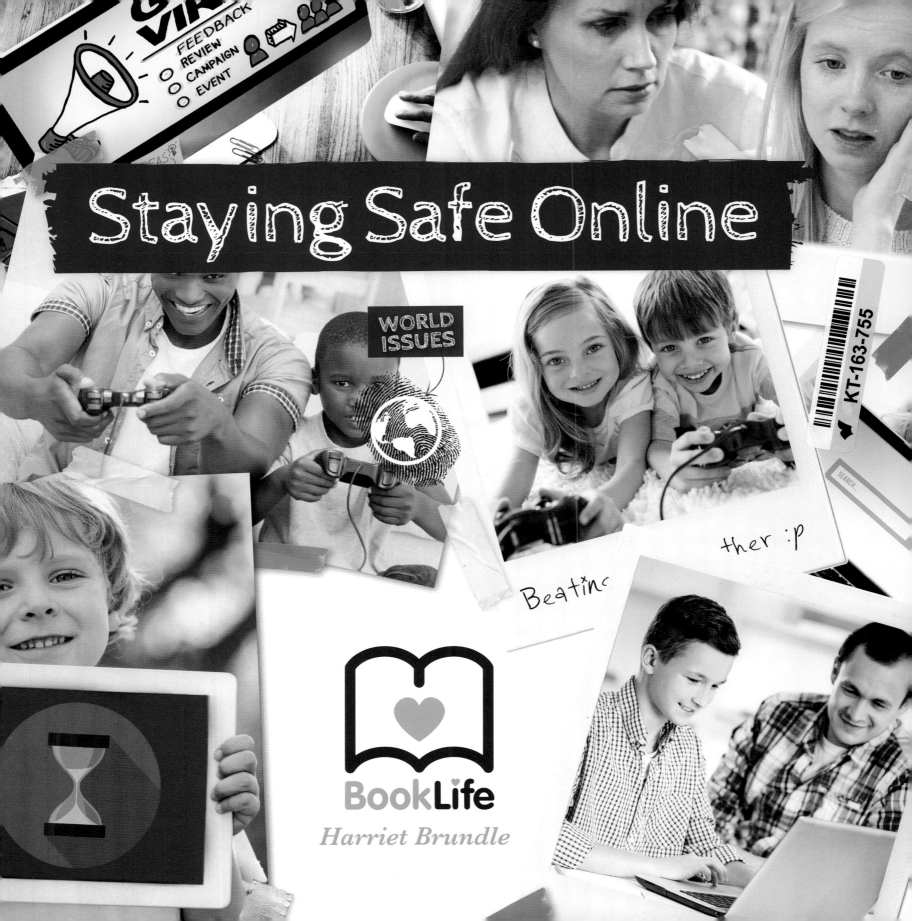

Staying Safe Online

WORLD ISSUES

KT-163-755

Beatinc

ther :p

BookLife

Harriet Brundle

WORLD ISSUES

©2016
Book Life
King's Lynn
Norfolk PE30 4LS

ISBN: 978-1-78637-023-5

©This edition was published in 2017.
First published in 2016.

Written by:
Harriet Brundle

Designed by:
Matt Rumbelow

A catalogue record for this book
is available from the British Library.

Contents

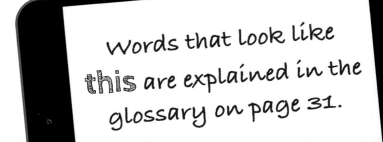

Words that look like *this* are explained in the glossary on page 31.

Words that look like *this* are important words.

What Does Online Safety *Mean?*

The ***internet*** is a fun, useful and informative resource that is used by people all around the world. We use the internet to access the ***World Wide Web*** (www.), which is made up of millions of different websites. Websites are used for a huge range of things, including communication, shopping, gaming and researching information.

We also use the internet to send messages to each other through email. This method of communication is much quicker than posting a letter!

The word 'internet' refers to the computer network that allows computer users to connect to each other. When a person is using the internet, they are ***online***.

Although the internet is extremely useful and continues to shape the way we live, it can also be dangerous and so it is extremely important to understand how to be safe while online.

Did you know? Over three billion people around the world use the internet!

3,000,000,000

The internet can be accessed from a range of different devices, including mobile phones, tablets and computers. On each of these devices, parental controls can be put in place to ensure the internet is safe for young people to use.

Don't forget to check with your parents that any devices you use have the right parental controls set up.

Why Is It Important to Stay Safe Online?

Unlike speaking to somebody face-to-face, we often cannot see who we are talking to over the internet. This means that a person you make friends with might not be who they say they are.

Five percent of teenagers who use the internet have admitted to arranging a secret meeting with somebody they met online.

It's important to never agree to meet somebody by yourself if you have made friends with them online. If you would like to meet a friend you met on the internet, always take a responsible adult with you and arrange a meeting place where plenty of other people will be around.

Not being able to see the person you are speaking to can also make some people say or do things they usually wouldn't do. They might say nasty or critical things that can be extremely upsetting for the person reading the comments.

It's important to remember that if someone says something online that upsets you, you must tell a responsible adult, for example your teacher. They will be able to help you to deal with the situation.

Sometimes people behave differently online from how they behave in person. This is called the *Online Disinhibition Effect*.

7

It is extremely important to remember not to share details about yourself with anybody online. Details such as your full name, your address or where you go to school are private. If a person asks you for this information, they might use it for other reasons than to get to know you as a friend.

If you create an online profile of any kind, make sure that you don't include any personal information. Ask an adult to check any pictures that you decide to upload to make sure they are suitable.

Fact! Every second, over 750 photos are uploaded to Instagram.

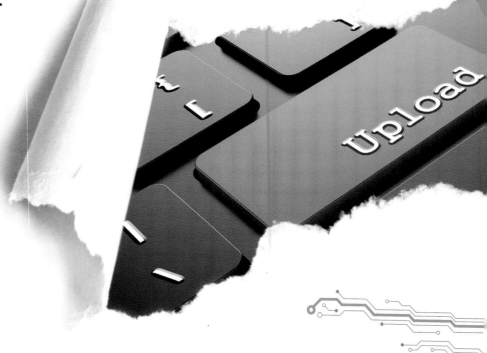

Many of the websites, games and social media sites that are on the internet will contain information, videos or images that are not suitable for children. Some of these sites could contain things younger people may find scary or upsetting.

Find out more about online gaming on page 18.

It's important to always check the age **restriction** before playing a game or watching a video online in order to to make sure the content is suitable for you.

Did you know? Over one hundred and seventy million copies of the violent shooting game series Call of Duty have been sold around the world. There are restrictions on these games stating that they shouldn't be played by people under the age of sixteen or eighteen. However, people much younger than this often play the games.

Social Media

The term **social media** refers to the online communication channels that allow people all over the world to create and share information, pictures and videos. Some of the most popular forms of social media are Facebook, Twitter and Instagram.

Be careful! Before you post something on social media, let an adult check your post to make sure that it does not put you at risk.

New Facebook Account!

Although social media offers a fun platform from where you can keep in touch with your friends, there are important things to remember in order to be safe.

If you want to use social media, don't forget to first check with a responsible adult and make sure you are old enough to create a profile.

10

Creating a secure password that cannot be easily guessed by others is very important. Try not to choose things like names of pets, friends or family and make sure the password you do choose includes a range of letters, numbers and punctuation.

Some social media sites also offer the option of private messaging. It's important that you only engage in private messaging with people that you know.

Remember never to share your password with anybody else, apart from the adults who look after you. If you share your password, you might be at risk of others logging into your account and doing things you don't want them to do.

A person who secretly gets access to a computer to cause damage or get information is a called a **hacker**.

Cyber Bullying

Cyber bullying is any form of bullying behaviour that is done online. Sadly, most young people will experience cyber bullying themselves, or see it being done to somebody else. One of the most common platforms for cyber bullying is social media sites.

A person who uses the internet to upset others or start arguments can be referred to as an **internet troll**.

Nearly 43% of children have experienced cyber bullying.

Many different things count as cyber bullying, including unkind comments, spreading rumours, impersonating somebody online, posting somebody else's personal information or uploading pictures that might make someone upset.

If you experience any kind of cyber bullying, it's very important to report it to a responsible adult, for example a parent or teacher, who can deal with the problem for you. If cyber bullying becomes extreme, the police can also become involved.

Other ways to stop cyber bullying include blocking the bully so they cannot contact you. Most social network sites also have a "report" option, so the person who posted what has upset you will receive a warning and the post will be removed.

Remember! Once something has been posted, even if deleted afterwards, it may have been printed or recorded by somebody else. Before you say or do something online, stop to think about how other people might feel.

13

Viruses

A virus is a particular type of program that is harmful to computers and other devices. Once a virus program is **activated**, the device becomes infected. Viruses can enter your device in lots of different ways. For example, you might receive a message encouraging you to click on a link and when you open the link, the virus enters your device.

Viruses come in lots of different forms but most are intended to cause harm, for example by stealing personal information.

Viruses are made by people all around the world. They are created for lots of different reasons, including making money.

Before you open a link or download any information, it's important to look at where it came from. Do you recognise the email address or the name of the person who sent it to you? If it's not somebody you know, it's likely to be a virus. Never click on a link or download something if you're unsure what it is. Speak to a responsible adult and ask them to check it first.

If you think you might have opened a virus on a device, tell an adult straight away so they can help.

Remember! Check with the person who looks after you to make sure that every device in your home has anti-virus software set up.

15

YouTube

The website YouTube was launched in 2005 and is used to share and watch videos. Now it is one of the most popular websites and over one hundred hours of video are uploaded to YouTube every minute!

The videos on YouTube cover a huge variety of subject areas, ranging from impressive football skills to amusing animals. The wide range of material available makes YouTube a great resource for finding information or learning new skills.

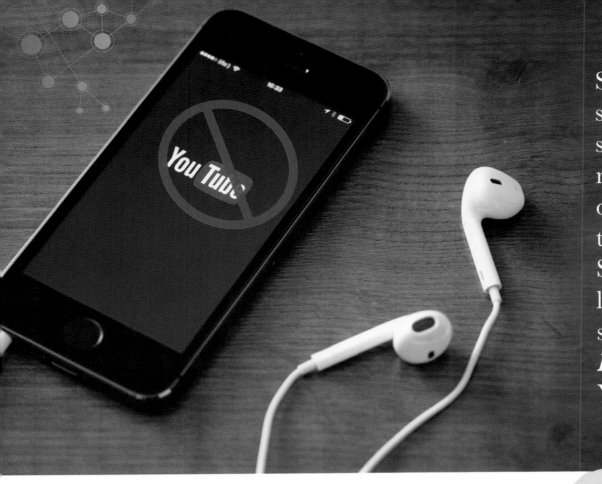

Some videos are not suitable for young people, so it is important that the right filters have been put on to the device you use to access the internet. Speak to whoever looks after you to make sure they have set up **_Restricted Mode_** on YouTube.

As YouTube offers such a wide range of videos and is used by so many people, it's important to make sure that you're careful about both what you watch and what you upload.

Once a video has been posted, you don't know who will see it. If you want to upload a video to YouTube, ask an adult to check that it doesn't contain anything that could put you at risk.

17

Online Gaming

An **online game** is a game that is played over to the internet. There are too many online games to count and new games are being created every minute!

Gamers can also use headsets whilst they play, which allows them to speak to whoever they are playing with at that time.

Beating my Brother :p

A new type of online gaming began when those using consoles, such as Xbox and PlayStation, were able to connect to each other via the internet. This allowed people to create teams with or play against people from all around the world.

Over one billion people use online games!

Connecting to others can be a great experience; however, it can lead to the other people you are playing with criticising you or saying unkind things that could be upsetting. If this happens, turn off your device and be sure to make an adult aware.

Try to set limits on the amount of time spent using online games and the internet more generally. If you need help to set a limit, speak to your parents and agree an amount of time you are all happy with. Although it may seem fun to play online for long periods of time, it's important to have other hobbies too.

Be careful! You won't always know who you are talking to or who you are playing with when using online games. The same rules apply when you are playing online games as when you are using social media.

Digital Footprint

Each time a person uses the internet, they leave a *digital footprint* behind. The footprint is the traces or trails of everything the person has done, including the websites used, what they have done on social media, their downloads and uploads.

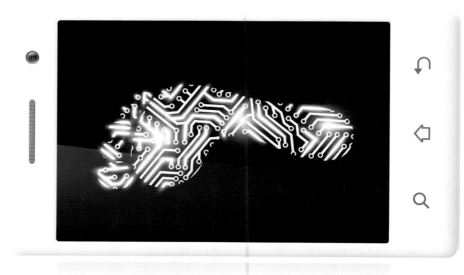

The easiest way to access digital footprints is by using a search engine to find someone. The results could be used for anything from companies researching a person before they offer them a job to the police tracking criminal activity.

Try this! Type your name into any online search engine and see what comes up. You may be surprised how much information you find!

A different way to see your digital footprint is to view the internet history on your device. This shows everything you have done online since using it, but it will not show things you have done online on other devices.

Most importantly, before you do anything online, think about how your actions could look to others if they were to see your digital footprint.

Even if you delete something, it may take some time for search engines to be updated so if you're unsure about whether to do something, make sure you think twice.

Online Safety and the Law

It is important to understand the difference between *illegal* and *offensive* online material. Everybody has different views and opinions that may conflict with your own. They may be offensive to you, but each person has a right to express how they feel, within reason.

Always think about how others may feel about what you're posting before you do it.

Illegal content is very serious and is dealt with by the authorities. This can include things such as hate speech, for example racism.

Remember! Make sure you have the correct safety controls set up on your device so that illegal content will not be shown.

If you feel you have seen something illegal online, it is very important to tell a responsible adult or report it directly to an authority such as the police.

Information can be reported **anonymously**.

Other ways of reporting illegal material include via charity run organisations. The ***Internet Watch Foundation*** or IWF is a charity that was started in 1996. It offers a safe and secure way for illegal online content to be reported. The IWF works with both the police and the government to make the internet a safer environment for everyone.

There are other charities that offer opportunities for people to report online issues, such as INHOPE. Search for them online!

Case Study: Cyber Bullying

Person Profile

Name: **Jessica**

Age: **10**

Problem:
Cyber Bullying

Jessica says "Rachel keeps sending me unkind online messages that are making me upset. If I post anything on Instagram she keeps making nasty comments that embarrass me and then shares what she has done so other people in our class can see. We used to be friends; I don't know why she is being such a bully."

What did Jessica do next?

"I decided the best thing to do was tell my teacher about what Rachel was doing. I showed my teacher the unkind messages and asked for it to be stopped. After I had shown my teacher the messages, I switched off my tablet so I didn't have to see it anymore."

Person Profile
Name: **Rachel** Age: **10**
Problem: **Cyber Bully**

Rachel says "I just thought it was funny to send Jessica messages, I didn't think she would actually get upset. I shared some of her pictures where I'd made funny comments so that other people would laugh too."

What happened?

"Our teacher told me that Jessica reported that I had been cyber bullying her! I didn't realise what I'd been doing was making her feel upset. I have spoken to Jessica and said sorry. I have deleted all the comments I made on Jessica's Instagram and will be much more careful in future."

Did You Know?

In 2013, a teacher in America was looking for the best way to show her students how quickly information can be shared once posted on the internet. She took a picture of herself holding a sign that explained she was talking to her students about how quickly a photo can be seen by lots of people and then posted the image on a popular social media site.

The teacher asked for those who saw the picture online to "like" it. Within just a few days, the picture had been "liked" by over six hundred thousand people!

I'm talking to my 5th grade students about internet safety and how quickly a photo can be seen by lots of people. If you are reading this, please click "LIKE." THANKS!

The picture was also shared by thousands of different people. This means that even if the teacher wanted to delete the post on her own social media profile, the image would not disappear from social media as it has been shared by others on their own profiles.

When something online, for example a picture or video, becomes extremely popular or spreads very quickly, it is said to have gone *viral*.

This teacher proved to her students that anything posted online is no longer private, you never know who may see it and you may never be able to delete it.

The Golden Rules of Online Safety

1 Remember that not everyone online is who they say they are.

2 Never meet with somebody you have met online, unless you have a responsible adult with you and have agreed a meeting place that is in a public area.

3 Never give out any personal information. This includes your address or which school you go to.

4 Make sure any device you use has the correct restriction controls set up. If you're unsure whether your device has the correct controls, speak to a parent or guardian.

5 Be very careful about posting pictures or videos of yourself online. Once you have posted something, it is no longer private and anybody could see it, share it or make a record of it.

6 Remember not to open any links or emails from people you don't know.

7 If you are experiencing cyber bullying or you have seen something upsetting or worrying online, tell an adult, report the incident or block the person responsible and turn off your device.

8 Remember that everything you do online leaves a digital footprint behind.

9 Always keep your passwords totally private, change them regularly and make sure they include letters, numbers and punctuation.

10 Most importantly, remember that the internet is an incredibly useful resource and, if used properly and safely, it can be both informative and fun!

Activity

Each of these key terms has a matching **definition** in the list below.
Can you match up each word with the correct definition?

Hacker

Internet Troll

Online Disinhibition Effect

Cyber Bullying

Online Game

Social Media

Digital Footprint

The traces or trails of everything a person has done whilst online

A game that is played whilst connected to the internet

Online communication channels that allow people all over the world to create and share information, pictures and videos

A person who secretly gets access to a computer to cause damage or get information

Any form of bullying behaviour that is done online

A person who uses the internet to upset others or start arguments

When people online behave in a way that they usually wouldn't if they were face-to-face with a person

Glossary

activated started

anonymously when something is done without giving your name

communication the passing of information between two or more people

conflict clash or be incompatible with

critical expressing a disapproval of something

definition the meaning of a word

devices objects designed for a particular purpose, usually machines

impersonating pretending to be someone else

parental controls online restrictions that are put in place by a parent or guardian

restriction a limiting condition or measure

websites pages of information on the internet

Index

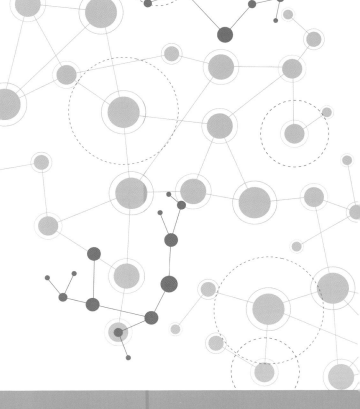

Credits

Photocredits: Abbreviations: l-left, r-right, b-bottom, t-top, c-centre, m-middle.
All images are courtesy of Shutterstock.com.

Front Coverbl – ISchmidt. br – VGstockstudio. ml – wavebreakmedia. mr – wavebreakmedia. tl – Rawpixel.com. tr -SpeedKingz. 2 – Andrey_Popov. 3 – guteksk7. 4tl-Andresr. 4bl – guteksk7. 4br – camilla$$. 5tr – wavebreakmedia. 5bl – Zaikina. 6b – Archiwiz. 6ml – Monkey Business Images. 6r – Africa Studio. 7tr – Monkey Business Images. 7bl – Syda Productions. 7br – guteksk7. 8tl – Andrey_Popov. 8bl – tanuha2001. 8br – Africa Studio. 9tr – best pixels. 9b – Veronica Louro. 10r – VGstockstudio. 10bl – Twin Design. 11tr – Ditty_about_summer. 11ml – Peter Kotoff. 11br – Gang Liu. 12r – oliveromg. 12bl – Gl0ck. 13tr – SpeedKingz. 13bl – Naruedom Yaempongsa. 14r – Georgejmclittle. 14br – frank_peters. 15tr – Samuel Borges Photography. 15bl – Monkey Business Images. 16tl – Alexey Boldin. 16br – Ronnachai Palas. 17t – Bloomua. 17br – guteksk7. 17bl – Creativa Images. 18bl – Siwasan Chiewpimolporn. 18r – wavebreakmedia. 19tr – wavebreakmedia. 19bl – Bloomua. 20tr -macro-vectors. 20bl – Syda Productions. 21tl – ISchmidt. 22tr – AntoinetteW. 22bl – Shyamalamuralinath. 23tr – Goodluz. 23bl – tanatat. 24lm – TijanaM. 25tr – tanatat & TijanaM. 25br – Anton Gvozdikov. 26bl – rangizzz. 27tr – Rawpixel.com. 27bl – Szasz-Fabian Ilka Erika. 28t – AlexandrBognat. 29br – stockyimages.